CURIOUS CREATURES

A PORTRAIT OF THE ANIMAL WORLD

Andrew Cleave

TODTRI

This book was designed and published by
TODTRI Book Publishers
254 West 31st Street, New York, NY 10001-2813
Fax: (212) 695-6984
E-mail: info@todtri.com

Visit us on the web!
www.todtri.com

Printed and bound in Indonesia

ISBN 1-880908-29-8

Author: Andrew Cleave

Publisher: Robert M. Tod
Book Designer: Mark Weinberg
Photo Editor: Edward Douglas
Editors: Don Kennison, Shawna Kimber
Production Co-ordinator: Heather Weigel
DTP Associate: Jackie Skyroczky
Typesetting: Command-O, NYC

PHOTO CREDITS

Photographer/Page Number

Dembinsky Photo Associates
John Gerlach 24-25
Gary Meszaros 4, 56-57
Stan Osolinski 28, 30, 66

Innerspace Visions
Doug Perrine 5, 53, 60
Ron & Valerie Taylor 32 (top)

Joe McDonald 26 (top), 29, 40 (top left), 64 (bottom), 68, 77 (bottom)

C. Allan Morgan 64 (top)

Nature Photographers Ltd.
S. C. Bisserot 34
Hugh Miles 59
O. Newman 35 (bottom)
Paul Sterry 54, 58, 69, 70

Picture Perfect USA
Mark Hanlon 23
Warren Jacobi 3

Edward S. Ross 8-9, 19 (bottom), 31, 39 (bottom), 40 (bottom left), 40-41, 44 (top),
45 (bottom), 51 (top), 55, 71, 73 (top right), 74 (top & bottom), 75 (top & bottom)

Leonard Lee Rue III 67 (bottom), 72-73

Gail Shumway 19 (top), 20 (top), 21, 38, 39 (top), 47 (top), 50, 51 (bottom)

Mary Snyderman 12 (top)

Tom Stack & Associates
Dave Fleetham 47 (bottom), 48 (top & bottom), 62 (bottom)
Warren Garst 77 (top)
Thomas Kitchin 15 (bottom)
Randy Morse 22
Brian Parker 13, 15 (top), 46, 56 (bottom left)
Rod Planck 73 (bottom right)
Ed Robinson 14 (top), 43
Mike Severns 14 (bottom), 27 (top), 42
Roy Toft 10, 11 (top), 37
Dave Watts 52

The WaterHouse
Stephen Frink 18

The Wildlife Collection
Gary Bell 27 (bottom), 33
John Giustina 6, 11(bottom), 35 (top), 56 (top left), 76
Martin Harvey 7, 26 (bottom), 67 (top), 79
Henry Holdsworth 65
Chris Huss 12 (bottom), 16, 17, 20 (bottom), 32 (bottom)
Tim Laman 36, 49, 61
Charles Melton 44 (bottom)
Robert Parks 45 (top)
Gary Schultz 78
Jack Swenson 62 (top), 63

INTRODUCTION

The markhor is the largest member of the goat family and surely one of the strangest in appearance. It is found in the mountains of south-west Asia and the males are characterised by long, straight and twisted horns and thick leg hair, forming what look like pantaloons.

"And now, worshipper of final causes and the mere useful in nature, answer but one question—why this prodigal variety?"

GLAUCUS BY CHARLES KINGSLEY, 1855

Evolution has produced many curiosities in the animal kingdom—creatures with strange shapes, creatures that look frightening yet are unable to cause any harm, creatures with incredible colourings and markings, and creatures that mimic each other or that don't even look like animals at all. In the animal kingdom every form of behaviour and every facet of an animal's structure and shape is there for a reason.

An animal may have evolved to blend in with its environment, like the fish of the Sargasso Sea, which are almost indistinguishable from the floating seaweed that covers the surface of its habitat. Similarly, an animal may display brilliant colours which make it stand out from its surroundings; here its appearance may serve as a warning to other creatures that this animal is poisonous or can cause some kind of harm. To our eyes an animal may have the most beautiful of markings, and these may be simply a characteristic to help camouflage it or attract a mate.

Whatever its appearance—however strange, frightening, or beautiful—there is undoubtedly a reasonable explanation for

the animal looking as it does. Our interest lies in discovering and understanding the appearance and resultant behaviour of these animals.

In the study of animal behaviour it is tempting to attribute to them human emotions. Anthropomorphism, the term used to describe the ascription of human characteristics to animals, is not uncommon with scientists as well as lay people. If a person runs away from a barking dog, it is said to be due to fear. There are recognisable signs of this fear: colour draining from the face, increased heart rate, sweating, and hair standing on end.

Similar physiological changes occur in animals—a cat's hair stands on end, for example, if it is confronted by the same barking dog and naturally the cat flees from danger. Could the emotion of fear be applied to the cat as well? The major difference between a cat and a human is that whilst both will flee from the dog a human, of course, is capable of thinking about the situation and perhaps assessing the consequences of different forms of reaction.

The cat's response is primarily instinctual, and although it may be able to learn from its experience and avoid dogs in the future it does not have the powers of reasoning a human employs. This is understood. However, odder aspects of an animal's behaviour will inevitably intrigue us. And when we are unable to explain rationally what an animal is doing we often attribute to it human traits—however erroneous they may be. Only careful and painstaking study will reveal the true meaning of an animal's behaviour.

The pink and maroon colours of this cleaner shrimp perfectly match the hues of the sea anemone on this reef off the Bahamas upon which it rests. This intriguing crustacean cleans visiting fish of parasites, performing a useful role in the coral reef community.

The giant water beetle, a voracious predator, will tackle almost anything its own size and sometimes even larger. This one is in the process of consuming a salamander larva, aided by tightly-gripping front claws and sharp jaws.

STRANGE BEAUTY

"When we once realise that whether in attacking or avoiding an enemy it is in most cases a great advantage to all animals to be hidden from view, and that each creature has arrived at this advantage by slow inheritance, so that their colours often exactly answer this purpose, how wonderful becomes the grey tint of the slug, the imitation of bark in the wings of the buff-tip moth, the green and brown hues of the eatable caterpillars, the white coat of the polar bear and the changing coat of the Arctic fox as winter comes on!"

WINNERS IN LIFE'S RACE BY ARABELLA BUCKLEY, 1882

An animal's appearance has much to do with its way of life. No feature on the body of an animal is there simply as adornment and no patch of colour or set of markings will be produced but for a specific reason. To gain an idea of the reasons behind an animal's appearance it is important to study the animal in its natural surroundings and if possible whilst it is unaware of being observed.

Many birds have brilliant colours and extravagant plumes or crests. They may sometimes be so elaborate that they appear to prevent the bird from flying or feeding without great difficulty. If the birds are observed in an aviary or especially if they are seen in illustrations against a blank page of a book the colours seem to be particularly striking. If, however, these same birds are seen against

Following page: The bright colours of this southern African locust advertise the fact that it has an unpleasant taste and is best avoided by predators. This one is eating euphorbia, a source of many foul-tasting chemicals.

Silhouetted against an African sunset these giraffes are amongst the most unmistakable of the continent's large mammals. Its long neck enables the giraffe to reach leaves and branches out of range of all other grazing animals.

The horns of the Nubian ibex are incredibly long and recurved, giving the animal a noble appearance. The horns are used not only in defence against predators but also in combat duels between rival males battling for the right to mate.

nature's background the colours appear more subdued and blend in well with each bird's surroundings.

Tropical Colours

Toucans are large colourful birds which inhabit the dense tropical forests of South America where there are patches of brightly coloured flowers and fruits and where the sunlight filtering through the many shades of green in the leaf canopy creates a variety of lighting effects. With its multicoloured plumage the toucan can easily

Few birds possess a larger or more striking bill than the saddle-billed stork from East Africa. Its colours complement the black-and-white plumage of the bird and provide attraction when pairs are displaying.

Like most other members of its family, this Sulawesi hornbill has a large protuberance, or casque, on the top of its bill. Although hard and rigid, the casque is honeycombed and air-filled inside; it helps resonate the bird's loud calls.

The large and colourful bill of the toco toucan is used in display. More important, it is used on a daily basis when feeding; its length allows the bird to obtain fruits and seeds otherwise out of reach.

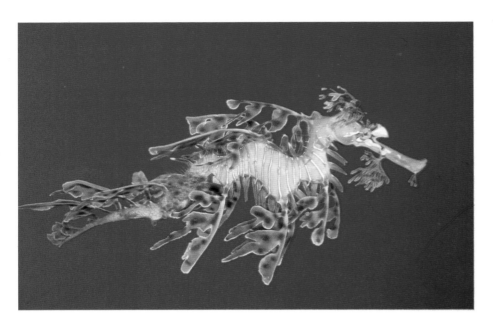

possibly warns off competitors of the same species.

The large bill of the toucan is used to cope with the hard shells of fruits and seeds, of course, but it also serves as part of the bird's display. It is normally a very colourful structure and by holding it in different positions the bird can indicate its intentions, showing aggression or perhaps readiness to mate.

Hornbills, the toucan's counterpart in the Old World, also have large, strikingly coloured bills which have evolved to aid in the bird's courtship display.

Bold Designs

Many fish have beautiful shapes and colours. As animals that are able to see in colour themselves their markings are an aid to attract others of the same species. Recognising others of your own species in the multi-coloured world of a coral reef is easier if patterns are bold and distinctive.

It may be an advantage to be completely hidden, however. Some fish, like the leafy sea dragon of the South Pacific, do their best to appear as one with their environment—in this case to look like floating sea-

An aptly-named leafy sea dragon, found in Spencer Gulf, Australia, floats buoyantly in the water, its extraordinary appearance affording it superb camouflage amongst floating seaweed. Even the most outrageous model maker could not have designed a more fantastic fish.

blend into its background, but if it wants to attract the attention of a mate it can use its colours to good effect by sitting out on a prominent branch and perhaps performing a display dance or making loud calls. Its appearance not only helps attract a mate but

With its intricate markings, strange shape, and projections, this Merlet's scorpion-fish could easily pass for colourful seaweed or coral. It goes without saying that, in the right setting, the animal's shape and colour afford it excellent camouflage.

This colourful seahorse does indeed have an equine profile. Seen out of context, its bright yellow colouring stands out but in its natural home amongst seaweeds and corals it blends in surprisingly well.

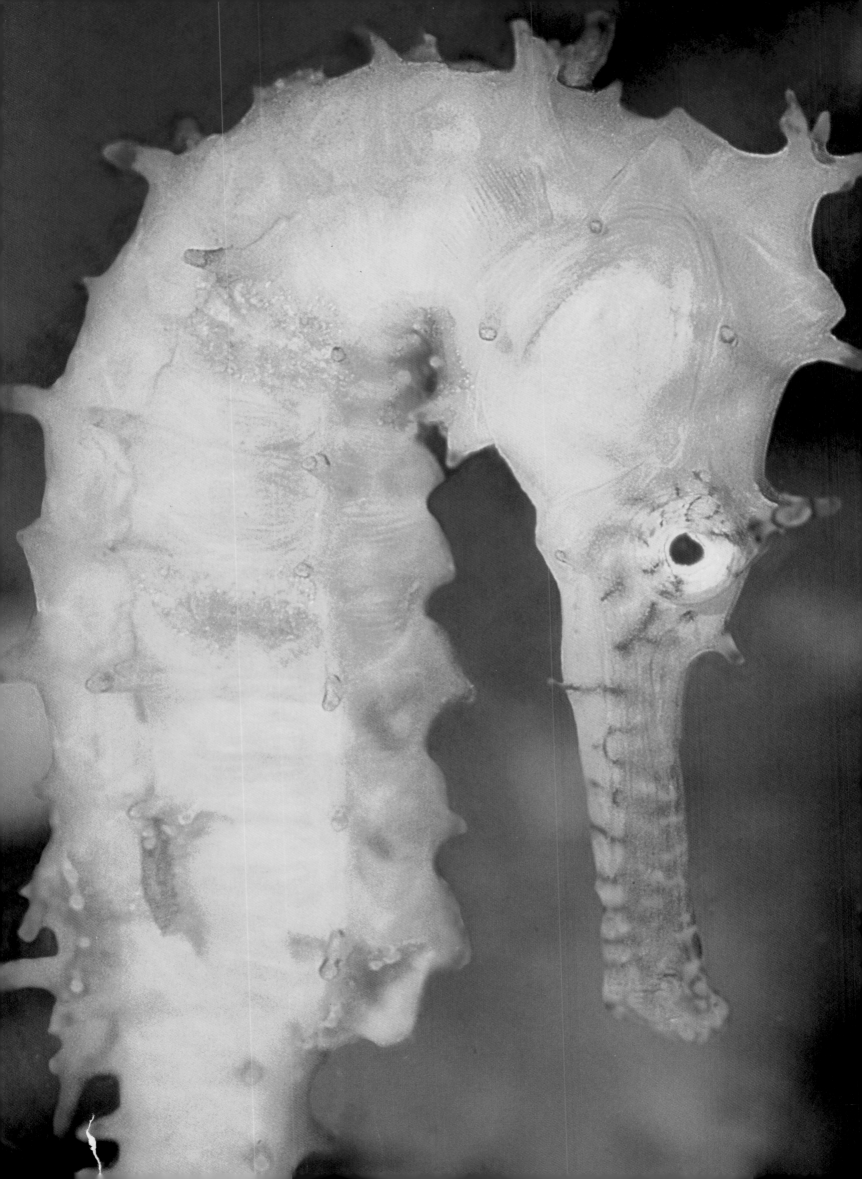

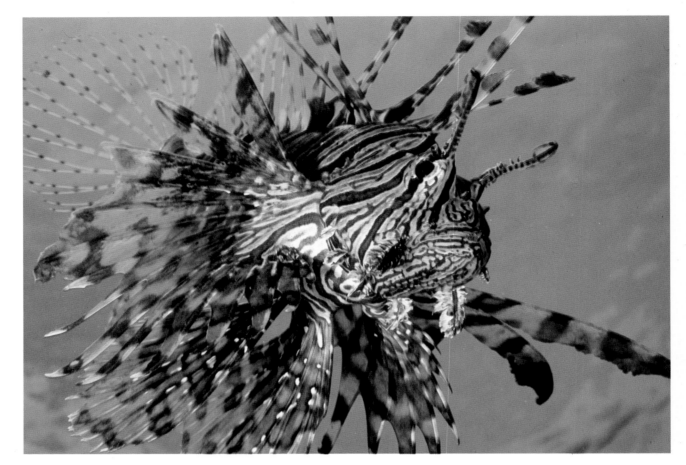

With fins elongated and splayed, this New Guinea turkey fish ripples and undulates even whilst hanging motionless in the water. Concealed within the seemingly delicate appendages are poison-tipped spines.

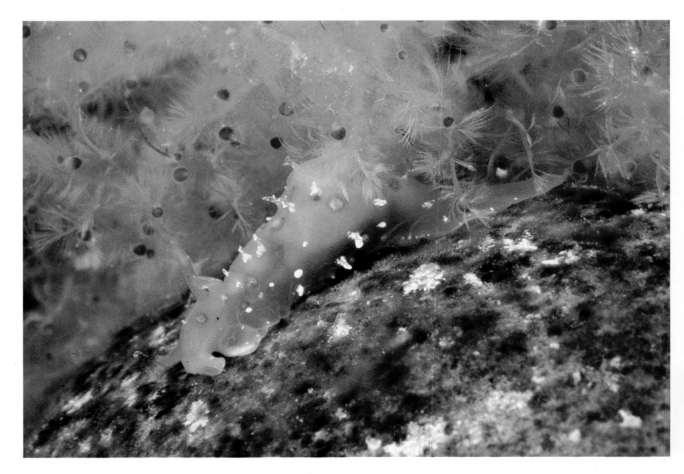

Working on the assumption that it pays to advertise, this orange and pink sea slug glides along slowly but confidently. The creature feeds on hydroids and sea anemones and is able to incorporate their stinging cells into its own skin for defence.

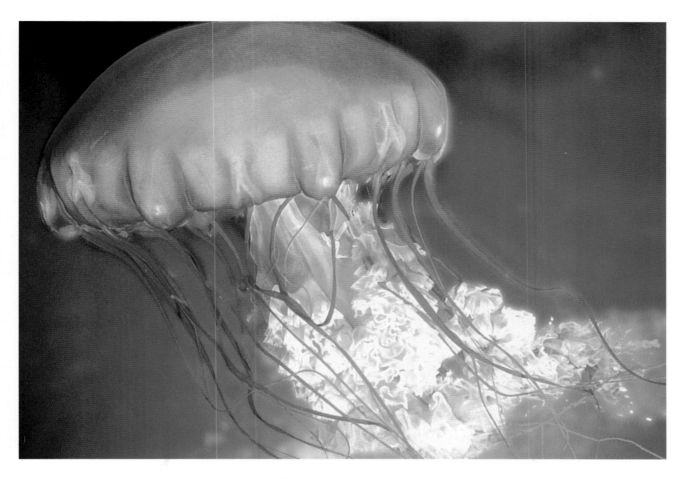

Beautiful but deadly, a jellyfish swims through the sea. The long fringe of orange tentacles trailing from the animal's umbrella-shaped body are armed with vicious stinging cells.

The subtle colouration found in nature is often stunningly beautiful. The soft pink tentacles of this pink-tipped sea anemone belie the fact that they are covered with deadly stinging cells.

weed. A sea dragon's fins are flattened and branched to resemble the fronds of seaweed and the fish even behaves like seaweed by swaying gently in the current in time with the actual seaweed around it. Only when placed in open water, away from any confusing background, can its true shape and form be discerned.

Sea horses, despite their common name, are indeed fish. They have uniquely shaped heads, and their tiny mouths are used to suck in small shrimps and fish fry. Their almost rigid bodies and curled, strong tails hold them in position amongst corals and seaweeds where they are very difficult to see; only as they move out into the open—infrequently, because this exposes them to danger—do they become at all conspicuous.

Despite having the name of an attractive flower, sea anemones are in fact animals. They are amongst the most attractive of all marine organisms, displaying flowerlike shapes and beautiful colourings. Their beauty is deceptive, however, for the gently waving tentacles, resembling the petals of a flower, are armed with stinging cells capable of killing small fish and shrimps, the staple diet of most sea anemones. Smaller animals, lured by its colours and movements, will be trapped and drawn into the anemone's hidden mouth, located in the centre of the rings of tentacles, to be slowly digested in the body cavity.

Jellyfish too have a delicate appearance which masks a mass of deadly stinging cells, some so powerful that they can inflict burning wounds even on human skin. Strangely, a few species of fish and shrimps seem to be immune to the poisons produced by anemones and jellyfish, and they can live quite happily amongst the stinging cells. They may serve to lure others of their kind—those less fortunate, with little or no protection—into the danger zone where they will become easy prey.

This attractive echinoderm, known as a pincushion starfish for obvious reasons, is found in the warm waters that bathe the Hawaiian Islands. The same radial symmetry observed in conventional starfish can be seen in this species.

Tiny tube feet on the undersides of these gulf starfish enable them to move as if they are gliding. The five legs form a star-shaped pattern characteristic of the starfish group as a whole.

This lichen-mimicking katydid resides in tropical forests in Ecuador. Its camouflage is so good that when resting on tree trunks and branches it is almost impossible to see.

Clever Disguises

A growth of lichens on trees—a sign of clear, unpolluted air—offers a good hiding place for insects which can match their background. Many moths have superb camouflage and when at rest on lichen-covered bark are almost impossible to see. Other insects as well can mimic the appearance of lichens, remaining nearly invisible until they make a move.

The lichen katydid, a relative of crickets, has the perfect markings and body appendages to help it blend in with a background of lichens; only its rasping call gives away its location. The lichen mantis lies in wait on twigs for smaller insects to pass by. Keeping absolutely still is no problem for a mantis, and being invisible against the right

background results in the fact that no insect is safe from the mantis if it comes too close.

The appearance of an animal is clearly of great importance to its survival, yet its behaviour must match this appearance. Having superb camouflage is of little use to an insect that looks like a leaf but moves in a strange way or rests against an inappropriately coloured background, thereby drawing attention to itself.

A lichen-mimicking mantid uses its camouflage to avoid detection by its potential prey, which include other, smaller insects. Under most circumstances the mantid chooses to rest amongst those lichens to which its markings have so well adapted.

Waving in the currents of the sea like a mop of hair, this sea anemone from the Red Sea possesses hundreds of tentacles, each armed with a battery of stinging cells. Living amongst these potentially deadly tentacles are colourful clownfish, which are immune to the anemone's toxins.

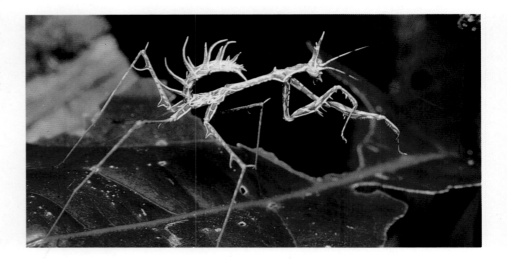

Although colourful and delightful to look at, these arrow poison frogs from Costa Rica are potentially deadly to anything that tries to attack them. Native Indians in the region use the frogs' poison on the tips of their arrows.

A writhing mass of ochre starfish illustrates the subtle variations in colour seen amongst members of the same species of many marine creatures. This species comes from North America's Pacific north-west.

Huge staring eyes dominate the head of this Brazilian tree frog and give it a certain functional elegance. Both its keen vision and the excellent grip provided by its sucker-tipped digits are required when leaping amongst rain-forest foliage.

FEARSOME CREATURES

". . . it has long given me deep pain when I have heard others stigmatising as ugly, horrid, or frightful, those beings whom their Maker saw at the beginning of the world, and declared very good. A naturalist will see as much beauty in a snake, spider, or toad as in any of those animals which we are accustomed to consider models of beauty."

THE BOY'S OWN BOOK OF NATURAL HISTORY BY REV. J. G. WOOD, 1900

Frightening away an enemy quickly and effectively is vital for some animals. If an animal is not big and strong, it could at least give the impression of great strength and deceive any adversary into leaving it alone. Many creatures, which in reality are quite small, can increase their apparent size by inflating their bodies with air or water, or by extending frills or appendages to make themselves appear much larger and more fearsome than they actually are.

The frilled lizard of Australia, for example, can fan out large flaps of scaly skin around its head so that when confronting an attacker head on it looks quite frightening. Its tiny body is hidden by the apparently huge head but most attackers will not stay around long enough to discover this for themselves.

The frightening appearance of the head end of the lizard can serve a further purpose. Rival

Following page: This Santa Fe land iguana is one of two species of land iguana unique to the Galápagos Islands. Because there are no native land predators on the islands this large lizard is indifferent to human onlookers.

Guaranteed to strike fear in the heart of any would-be predator, this frilled lizard from Australia spreads its neck flaps in full display. For its comparatively small size, the lizard is bold and pugnacious.

Few creatures on earth are more ugly and unappealing than the grotesque wolffish. It takes little imagination to realise that its sharpened teeth have earned the creature its name.

This warthog's tusks are not just for show. If cornered, the razor-sharp teeth can inflict severe, if not fatal, wounds on an attacker, and predators such as lions or leopards will think twice before tackling this creature.

Although its savage reputation exceeds the truth, the Tasmanian devil has been known to attack animals as large as sheep. It has an ill-tempered nature and an extremely powerful neck. Its snarling mouth reveals teeth that can inflict serious damage.

This large monitor lizard is on the prowl through the mangrove swamps of Indonesia. It will eat almost anything that it can catch, including small mammals, birds, and other reptiles.

Komodo dragons reach a length of 3 metres (10 feet), including the tail, and are large enough to take live prey such as wild pigs and occasionally humans. They are found only on the island of Komodo in south-east Asia.

males, competing for the attention of a female before mating, will threaten each other with their elaborate frills and the most impressive male wins the favours of the female.

Fear and Dominance

The Galápagos Islands, six hundred miles out in the Pacific Ocean off the coast of Ecuador, are home to many species of reptiles, amongst them the marine iguana, the only large lizard which regularly feeds under the sea. These iguanas can grow to lengths of around 1 metre (3 feet) and they are armed with tough, scaly skins, long claws, and a row of thick, sharp spines along the top of the body.

An interesting feature of the Galápagos Islands is their almost complete lack of land

Massed ranks of marine iguanas bask in the Galápagos Islands. Because they are cold-blooded, these unusual reptiles spend a good deal of their time sunbathing on the rocks in order to raise their body temperature.

This prehensile-tailed skink from the Solomon Islands is adept at climbing bushes and trees— its gripping tail acts as a fifth limb. The curiously shaped nostrils give the lizard something of a science-fiction appearance.

Although this bizarre creature resembles a dinosaur it is in fact alive and well and living in the Galápagos Islands. It is a marine iguana, an unusual lizard that grazes seaweeds on the seashore.

predators. Thus, there is little need for marine iguanas to possess defences against attack from other species. In fact, these creatures are so sure of their own safety that they will allow humans to approach them. Their gruesome appearance, therefore, is a physical trait that evolved to impress other iguanas.

Although the Galápagos Islands are on the equator and the air temperature can be very high during the day, the sea water is comparatively cool as a result of the cold current which sweeps up the coast of South America from the Antarctic. Thus, when the iguanas dive into the sea to feed on seaweed their bodies cool quite quickly. As cold-blooded creatures, they need to come out of the water

and bask in the sun to warm themselves up again; good basking sites are therefore very important to them and there is great competition to keep possession of the best spots. The more frightening an iguana looks, the better equipped it is to take hold and keep a prime site.

Found also on the Galápagos Islands is the land iguana, a similarly large lizard, but one that does not swim in the sea. It prefers to eat vegetation found on land and will guard a good feeding and sunbathing area. It lacks the array of spines found on the marine iguana but it does have a colourful body, and it will present this sideways to an attacker in order to make itself look larger. During courtship as well it is naturally the strongest-looking male that gets to mate.

Surviving Attack

Other land-dwelling lizards, such as monitors, rely on their great size to intimidate attackers and usually stand their ground when confronted, often adopting an aggressive posture. Some species use different parts of their bodies to ward off or confuse attackers. The tail may be specially modified with bright colours or a striking shape which will divert the attention of an attacker from its head. Flicking the tail or holding it menac-

ingly will also distract another animal.

If a lizard is attacked, regardless of such defences, the injured creature can afford a damaged tail as this is a part of the body that regenerates easily. A head-shaped tail, or at least a brightly coloured tail, will save vital organs, such as the actual head, from the damaging attack. If the tail breaks off during an attack and is left behind twitching and wriggling, the lizard can escape whilst the predator is thus distracted. Other defences like spines and thick scales all help to deter a predator, perhaps for a few vital seconds in which an escape can be made.

The spiny-tailed lizard from southern Africa carries upon its back its best means of defence— namely sharp, spiny scales. Those of the tail are particularly fearsome and can be lashed out if the creature is attacked.

Amongst diving circles, the hammerhead shark is one of the most feared of all fish. Although its unusual head shape may appear faintly comical, the bite it can inflict is very serious indeed.

Lurking at the opening to a crevice in a coral reef off Baja, California, this moray eel resembles a vision from hell. The array of needle-sharp teeth that adorn its mouth ensures that any victim has little chance of escaping its bite.

Marine Strategies

Many fish have no defence other than aggressive appearance and behaviour with which to scare off a predator. Moray eels are naturally aggressive creatures with strong, sharp teeth but their bodies are defenceless, lacking any tough outer scales. Normally they remain inside caves or burrows with only the head showing. By baring their teeth and filling the entrances to their hiding places with folds of their long body these eels can appear very frightening looking.

The body of an octopus may not be armoured or protected but this does not keep it from catching crabs and other shellfish with ease. Prey is gripped in the deadly embrace of its tentacles whilst sharp mouthparts deliver a poisonous bite.

Flying Terrors

Bats are largely misunderstood. Due primarily to the reputation of the vampire bat, all bat species are considered to be frightening creatures. Centuries of suspicion and ignorance colour people's ideas about them to this day.

Unfortunately, the strange appearance of most bats does little to improve their image. The long-eared bats of Europe have huge ear flaps, almost as long as their bodies, and on close examination their faces are quite extraordinary as well, possessing tiny eyes and large noses. All of these unusual facial features have in fact evolved to help the bat locate its food, which consists solely of night-flying insects.

Bats emit high-frequency sounds—inaudible to human ears—which send back echoes when they hit objects within range. These very high-pitched squeaks are easily picked up by the large ears which act as reflectors, enabling the bat to judge the exact position of a flying insect, such as a moth, in total darkness.

The vampire bat lacks the large ears of the long-eared bat because its prey is quite different. Although like most bats it feeds by night, it prefers something larger than a moth. It has developed a technique for sucking the blood of large mammals such as cattle.

When cows are ruminating quietly at night,

lying in a meadow for instance, the vampire bat will fly down and bite the cow's leg just above the hoof where blood vessels are close to the surface. The cow may feel a little irritation but it usually does not flinch, allowing the bat to drink its fill of fresh blood. The bat's teeth are sharp enough to penetrate the cow's skin but not so large that they cause pain and thus drive off its prey. Despite popular legends and myths, humans are normally not the victims of vampire bats.

The truth about the bats upon which vampire legends are based is almost stranger than the fiction. Using their sharp teeth the vampire bats make an incision in the skin of mammals and then feed on the blood.

A reason bats are so feared by some is their ability to fly in complete darkness. They utilise their echolocation capability in this feat; the large ears of this long-eared bat greatly assist in this process.

Bats have a unique stature in myths and folklore and are the stuff of vampire legends. This long-eared bat, whose diet is confined to night-flying moths and other insects, has a more agreeable appearance than others of its species.

Scary Scavengers

The strange appearance of vultures, characterised by their odd-looking bare skin, has more to do with their method of feeding than with scaring off potential predators. These very large birds perform a vital role as scavengers by clearing away the carcases of dead animals after primary predators have had their fill.

A vulture often pushes its head and neck into the carcase in order to rip out pieces of remaining flesh, and usually there are many vultures feeding at any given time. In their scramble for food, feathers would very quickly become soiled and then of course need to be cleaned; as a result vultures have dispensed with this common physical attribute of birds altogether. Some vultures have skin that is brightly coloured, in lieu of any colourings which would be present had they possessed feathers.

Only another king vulture could find this remarkable bird attractive! The strangely shaped nostrils at the base of the bill aid its greatly enhanced sense of smell; with it the vulture can detect a rotting corpse whilst flying high over South American rain forests.

A California condor, one of the last of its kind, displays its bare face and neck. A lack of feathering on these parts of the body allows vultures as well as condors to feed inside rotting carcase cavities without getting their plumage matted.

The head of this polyphemus moth, found in Florida, is extraordinary as seen in close-up. Two compound eyes stare out from its hairy features and are flanked by large, feathery antennae, part of the moth's sensory system, which help it detect airborne scents.

This female praying mantis from the Congo will defend her egg-mass with amazing vigour. The widely-spread front legs and the prospect of a painful bite are enough to deter most birds and other potential predators.

Mother spiders are renowned for the fearless way in which they defend their eggs and young. This green lynx spider from Florida is more than a match for most small predators and can inflict a painful bite in defence.

Parental care in the invertebrate world is uncommon but there can be few better exceptions than this scorpion. The female carries her young on her back for several weeks and will defend them to the death.

For most insects a tarantula spider is a deadly foe. Not so, however, for this predatory wasp known as a tarantula hawk, which can paralyse its victim with comparative ease. The spider's body then serves as a food supply for the wasp's young.

For any small insect, capture in the vicelike grip of a mantid is certain death. The sharp and powerful mouthparts make short work of this unfortunate locust.

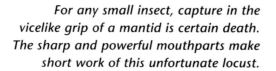

BIZARRE AND UNUSUAL CREATURES

"When we see any part or organ developed in a remarkable degree or manner in any species, the fair presumption is that it is of high importance to that species."

THE ORIGIN OF SPECIES BY CHARLES DARWIN, 1859

A coral reef provides plenty of opportunities for studying some of the more unusual members of the animal kingdom, for there are many examples here of plants and animals which are never quite what they seem to be at first glance.

The coral itself is an example of an animal that, while individually is very small and almost defenceless, when found in a colony of millions is capable of forming huge reefs with a rocklike structure. Many species of coral exist, some looking like plants and some looking like other members of the animal kingdom. Living amongst the coral are a multitude of animals with an equally varied set of shapes, sizes, colours, and habits.

With a face resembling extruded plastic, this frogfish is one of the ocean's more bizarre-looking fish. When resting amongst encrusted rocks and corals it is surprisingly well camouflaged.

Spot the fish! This frogfish was photographed on a coral reef off the coast of Hawaii. Not only does its colour scheme match its habitat, this extraordinary creature can successfully mimic the texture of the reef as well.

Insects are the only invertebrates capable of flight. Some are extremely skilled in this ability: this spider-fly from California, for example, is hovering in mid-air whilst using its proboscis to feed on nectar.

This glow-worm beetle is a formidable predator, armed as it is with powerful piercing and biting mouthparts as well as large, feathery antennae which enhance its ability to detect its prey.

Many insects such as butterflies and flies visit flowers to feed on nectar. Lying in wait for them is a favourite strategy amongst praying mantids, which grasp the unfortunate victim with their barbed front legs.

Long proboscislike mouthparts enable weevils to feed on plant juices from within fruit and sap. This Peruvian species also has incredibly long legs, which are flattened and colourful at their tips.

Camouflage

Fish are especially abundant on coral reefs and many of them blend in perfectly with their surroundings. Hawkfish are rather shy fish which remain perfectly still on an exposed perch, relying on camouflage to conceal them. Good eyesight enables them to spot an approaching small prey fish, for which they will dart out, rather as a bird of prey would, to catch their victim. On returning to their resting places they blend again into the background.

Many other fish have strange shapes or habits which make them resemble various members of the animal kingdom. The frogfish has a superficial resemblance to a frog, allowing it to remain out of view amongst rocks and corals. Similarly, the scorpionfish, although brightly coloured itself, becomes almost invisible against a background of coral. The crocodile fish of Indonesia has an elongated snout, bearing a slight resemblance to that of the reptile's, but this is an adaptation to feeding. The fish itself is quite difficult to see when resting quietly amongst the rocks and debris of its habitat.

Angular projections above the eyes earn this Asiatic horned toad its name. As it rests on the forest floor amongst dry leaves it can be extremely difficult to spot.

The hawkfish traps an unfortunate victim in its mouth. Backward-pointing teeth and strong jaws ensure that there is no escape.

Utilising its elongated snout, this long-nosed hawkfish applies its mouth like a pair of tweezers. It is thus able to pick morsels of food from crevices in the Hawaiian coral reef where it resides.

Looking like a brightly coloured, seaweed-encrusted rock, the titan scorpionfish is a master of disguise. If an unsuspecting smaller fish or shrimp swims close by, the scorpionfish will swallow it whole within its large gape. Scorpionfish are amongst the most poisonous fish in the sea.

As portrayed by its elongated snout, this Indonesian crocodile fish is indeed aptly named. Aided by excellent camouflage, it lies in wait for passing prey including smaller fish, which are then unhesitatingly snapped up.

Mantid species around the world are past masters at lying in wait, camouflaged amongst their surroundings. This species from southeast Asia looks for all the world like a dead leaf.

These strange-looking creatures are longhorn beetles, photographed in Yunnan, China. The feathery-tipped horns are in fact sensory antennae.

There can be few better examples of twig-mimicry than this arboreal snake from Madagascar. Even the colours and textures of the lichens are reproduced on its scales with faithful accuracy.

To some this Costa Rican katydid looks more like a sci-fi alien than an insect. The conical projection on its head has earned it the name of conehead; in addition to serving as a means of defence and acting as part of its camouflage, the cone gives the creature a strangely attractive appearance.

Strange Mammals

Most mammals have a fairly conventional and recognisable shape and appearance, but some at first glance almost defy classification. One of the most bizarre of all mammals is the duck-billed platypus of Australia. As an egg-laying mammal it is odd enough but more peculiarly this creature has what looks like a duck's beak instead of a nose or snout.

Indeed, when this animal was first discovered and skins were sent from Australia to museums in Europe, zoologists thought they were being fooled by a taxidermist's hoax. The platypus's skeleton shows many features similar to that of a reptile's skeleton, yet the young, having hatched from eggs, are covered with fur and are suckled with milk produced by the mother—two significant features of mammals. A platypus's mammary glands lack the teats found in the higher mammals but despite their primitive structure they do provide nourishment for the young.

The platypus has webbed feet with claws making it both a good swimmer and a strong climber, a great help when negotiating muddy river banks. The ducklike beak is used to sift through mud in search of worms, the staple food of the platypus.

Manatees seem to fit into no category of aquatic mammals. Obviously, they are not sleek, deep-diving, and fast-swimming like whales and dolphins, and they do not haul themselves out on land or catch fish like seals. They are in fact gentle plant-eaters. Their common name, 'sea cow', seems far more appropriate as they graze peacefully in shallow water, feeding on lush green aquatic vegetation. They are lovers of warm water and will spend long hours basking near the surface in shallow waters where the sun has warmed it.

There is a belief that manatees are the origin of the mermaid legends, but how the thick-skinned, small-eyed, bewhiskered visage of the manatee could be confused with the face of a supposedly beautiful creature, half human and half fish, is difficult to understand. These harmless creatures are endangered and becoming rare as a result of persecution and damage to their habitat by pollution and disturbance. Only in specially protected areas can manatees today be seen living out their peaceful lives.

At one time zoological authorities considered reports of the duck-billed platypus to be a hoax. Not only does this extraordinary mammal have a mouthpart which resembles that of a duck but it lays eggs as well.

Manatees live in the warm waters around the coast of Florida and the Caribbean. Sometimes known as sea cows, these gentle vegetarians feed on sea grasses and can reach a length of around 4 metres (12 feet).

Unforgettable Faces

A distinctive feature of the face of most mammals is the nose, and it is often one of the best ways of recognising individuals. Four unusual mammals have noses of great distinction, making them quite unmistakable. But you can be sure that the nose of the tapir, the proboscis monkey, the mandrill, and the star-nosed mole serves each a very useful purpose despite its bizarre appearance.

The tapirs of South America and Malaysia are primitive hoofed mammals that possess a trunklike snout formed by an extended upper lip. The nostrils at the end of this flexible snout are used to draw food, usually leaves and small twigs, into the mouth. Tapirs seem to have remained nearly unchanged during the course of evolution. Young tapirs have

striped markings to provide them with camouflage in dense forests, but they lose this feature as they grow older.

An adult tapir may grow to be around 2 metres (6 feet) long and is able to look after itself quite well. Tapirs are usually found near water and in damp areas of tropical forests; if alarmed they will often move into the water and remain submerged for several minutes. They lead very secretive lives and are difficult to observe in the wild.

The enormous, pendulous nose of the male proboscis monkey of Borneo gives it a very distinctive silhouette. This strange facial feature may help the male make its resonant honking call or it may simply increase its chances of winning battles over females by making it look more impressive. This is a difficult animal to watch closely in the wild as it is usually found high in the tree canopy. It may, however, sometimes be seen swimming across a stream.

The mandrill, a member of the baboon family, lives mainly near the West African coast, inhabiting forests where it feeds on fruits, berries, and other parts of plants. It is quite a good climber but normally remains on the forest floor. A dominant male will guard his troop of females and young from predatorial and rival male attacks by doing its best to look frightening.

Charging at an attacker with its brightly coloured nose set in a frightening face and a strangely hunched posture, the male man-drill will usually succeed in driving all but the bravest rival away. A further unusual feature of the mandrill is that its rear end is oddly coloured blue and white; thus when standing in a threatening posture it can advertise its aggression in either direction.

The star-nosed mole is odd in several ways but mainly because of the strange starlike arrangement of tentacles around its nostrils. These features are highly sensitive and help it to find food in darkness as well as in the muddy water in which it swims, readily using its almost flipperlike limbs to help it move. Like all moles it has an insatiable appetite for earthworms and its distinctive nose is an invaluable aid to finding them.

This two-headed gopher snake, the result of a developmental mutation, is the stuff of nightmares. In the wild, individuals with deformities such as this seldom survive for very long.

Male mandrills have extremely striking and colourful faces and rumps. The colours indicate the degree of dominance of a particular individual—the more intense the markings the more superior its position.

Although it resembles a pig, the tapir is in fact an ungulate and is related to horses. This particular species is found in swampy forests of South America. Timid and largely nocturnal, they are difficult to observe in the wild.

A star-nosed mole emerges from its burrow. The fleshy, fingerlike projections which surround its nose and mouth are used to detect food items such as earthworms and insects.

Flightless Birds

A feature of birds normally taken for granted is their ability to fly but some birds have lost this skill and remain on the ground. The ostrich, for example, is far too large to be able to lift itself and remain airborne. Its huge bulk would require vast wings and immensely powerful flight muscles for support.

It has instead transferred its energies to that of rapid running and can escape predators just as effectively as if it were capable of flight. Strong leg muscles and tough feet enable it to run at high speeds and over long distances across the plains of Africa. Males are distinctive black-and-white birds but females are plainer, with more restrained brownish colouration. They blend well into the background when laying their eggs, which to human eyes are extremely large.

Ostrich eggs are in fact simultaneously both the largest and smallest of bird's eggs. No other bird's egg is as large as the ostrich egg but in relation to the size of the bird that lays them they are in fact very small, which is why the female can produce clutches of ten or more quite easily. The eggs could not be much larger, though, for the shell would then be too thick, making it impossible for the chicks to break their way out when hatching.

The flightless cormorant of the Galápagos Islands has also lost the ability to fly, but this bird has transferred its skills to swimming. On these almost predator-free islands there is little need for the cormorant to fly. As long as it is able to get from its roosting and nesting sites to the sea without much difficulty, wings are no longer a necessity. As with all other flightless birds, the flightless cormorant has not lost its wings completely but they are greatly reduced in size. They are used only for balance as the cormorant hops over rocks on its way to the sea.

Rich feeding supplies in inshore waters and a lack of ground predators have resulted in the Galápagos Islands' flightless cormorants having lost the ability to fly. Their wings are reduced to tiny stumps.

A male ostrich, the largest bird in the world, guards his eggs and hatchlings. The clutch may comprise eggs laid communally by up to three females with whom he has mated.

STARTLING BEHAVIOUR

"Our attention has been directed in a particular manner to the various instinctive powers of animals—that hidden principal which actuates and impels every living creature to procure its subsistence, provide for its safety and propagate its kind."

A GENERAL HISTORY OF THE QUADRUPEDS
BY THOMAS BEWICK, 1807

The element of surprise is very important when making an attack, or when defending yourself, and those animals that may lack other defences, such as great strength or speed, will often rely on some startling form of behaviour to defend themselves. A sudden increase in size, a quick movement, or the appearance of death may serve to unsettle an attacker and help save the animal's life.

Defence and Escape

Fish apply many methods of defence and the puffer fish are amongst the most startling. Although relatively small, puffers can almost treble their size by inflating their bodies with water and becoming balloonlike in a very short time.

Some, like the spotted puffer, perform this in the open water but others may do it in a confined space such as a burrow, making it impossible for a predator to enter or to pull them out. The spotted puffer has additional methods of defence as it belongs to a family of fish which are able to release poisonous toxins to deter attackers.

The flying gurnard has greatly enlarged pectoral fins which when extended make the fish appear about three times its normal size. Their striking pattern of dark spots acts as a

Ever alert, these suricates work as a team in all aspects of life. Because they are vulnerable to attack from ground predators and birds of prey, there are always a few individuals on the lookout at any given time.

When threatened with attack, this puffer fish's defence is to inflate its body to an incredible degree. It then becomes almost the size of a football and thus an impossible prospect for most predators.

warning as the fish 'flies' rapidly away from danger. The flying fish of the Pacific also have large pectoral fins which help them glide above the waves and escape from larger hungry fish below. So good are they at skimming over the surface that flying fish sometimes find themselves on the decks of boats; having escaped from one predator they then might end up as a meal for the crew.

When danger threatens beneath the waves, flying fish can break through the surface of the sea and, using their enormously enlarged pectoral fins, catch the breeze and glide for hundreds of yards.

Striking Suitors

The enormous elephant seal is one of those creatures which combines great size and strength with aggressive behaviour and a startling display. This huge limbless animal lies on a beach looking quite incapable of rapid movement or of anything more strenuous than scratching itself with a flipper. If a rival animal approaches too closely, however, it will rear itself up, inflating its nostril pouches, and open a huge red mouth armed with vicious teeth. Loud bellowing sounds accompany this display and the whole performance is usually enough to intimidate all but the strongest and most aggressive rival.

Usually the threatening display is enough to make a rival back away but sometimes two rivals will make actual physical contact, often badly injuring each other and drawing blood in the process. Normally, though, these aggressive displays serve a very useful purpose in taking the place of physical battles and preventing large animals from badly injuring each other.

With enormously enlarged and flattened pectoral fins, this flying gurnard from Hawaii glides effortlessly over the sea bed. The markings on its fins afford the creature excellent camouflage whilst at rest.

Battling for supremacy and the right to mate with a harem of females, these male elephant seals are capable of inflicting severe wounds on one another. Males are much larger than females and can weigh as much as 1,800 kilogrammes (2 tons).

The behaviour of birds during courtship has long interested naturalists. Many species have evolved elaborate display rituals in order to impress others of their species. The male sage grouse of the dry grasslands of North America, for instance, displays itself by spreading out its tail feathers and puffing up its chest; this is accompanied by a strutting dance and loud calls designed to impress any onlooking females. Similarly, the male ostrich uses his black-and-white plumage to good effect in a stately dance in which he shows off his wings, useless for flight but ideal for impressing a more drably coloured female.

The blue-footed booby, like other members of the booby family, indulges in sky-pointing whilst sitting on its nest. This is a signal that the territory is occupied. In a crowded sea bird colony, where every nest site is fought over by rivals, signalling occupation is very important. There are very few differences in the physical appearance of the sexes in boobies so any signals that can be given to show a bird's intentions are very significant.

When not occupying their nesting sites the boobies may flock together in search of food. They are highly skilled at diving for fish just below the surface and if a shoal of suitable fish appears they will all dive, in a coordinated feeding frenzy, turning the water white with foam. Just as suddenly as the feeding frenzy starts it will finish and the flock of boobies will disperse until more food is found elsewhere.

The large marabou stork does not perform such lively displays as the ostrich or feed in as active a way as the boobies. It seems instead to spend much of its time sitting in a rather odd position. Its very long legs are typical of most storks but it has an unusual way of resting—it folds its legs back and sits on its ankles. Somehow it is able to get up from this position whenever it is ready to move off and feed again.

Blue-footed boobies are ever alert for feeding opportunities. If a shoal of fish ventures near the surface of the sea, scared, perhaps, by a predator beneath the waves, boobies congregate and dive in a feeding frenzy.

A displaying male sage grouse is an amazing sight. With air sacs inflated, he parades around making a loud and curious bubbling and popping sound.

Often likened to a group of undertakers awaiting clients, these marabou storks gather near a lion kill. Despite their size they are rather timid and will wait for the big cats to finish their meal before taking theirs, resting the while by folding their legs back and sitting on their ankles.

Like a bird turned flamenco dancer, a male ostrich performs his courtship dance. If the female—who is just out of camera shot—likes his display, mating will shortly follow.

Like a grim sentinel, a marabou stork stands aloft on a tall branch. These birds are scavengers and spend much of their time watching for signs of feeding activity amongst predators of the African plains.

Deception and Mimicry

Playing dead or mimicking an inanimate object is a good way of saving oneself from attack. Some harmless species of snake which lack venom or the strength to overcome an enemy will become limp and adopt the posture of a dead animal when under attack. Often it is resistance by the animal being attacked which leads to serious damage, but once it becomes lifeless its attacker will usually lose interest and move off. By rolling over and leaving its mouth agape the snake will have saved itself from further aggression.

The looper caterpillar, or inchworm, does its best to appear like a twig. Not only does it look like a twig it also acts like a twig—by holding its body stiffly away from the main twig at the correct angle. When it needs to move in search of food it does so by looping its body along the twig. At the first sign of danger, such as a sudden tap on the twig which may signal a hungry bird landing to feed, the looper will adopt its twiglike posture and freeze until it is safe to move again.

When escape is impossible and danger threatens, hognose snakes invariably play dead. This sham is often enough to fool most would-be predators, who are put off as well by an unpleasant smell emitted by the reptile.

Known as looper caterpillars in Britain and inchworms in North America, geometrid moth larvae move by looping their bodies along twigs. Most are extremely well camouflaged, as both their shape and their colour perfectly match the twigs on which they rest.

Beetle Behaviour

There are more species of insects in the world than any other type of animal, and of the insects beetles are the most numerous. New species are still being discovered in tropical forests and many of our well-known beetles are still providing us with interesting insights into their way of life.

Most freshwater ponds have numerous beetles living in them, including the predatory diving beetle. The large, glossy green and gold, great diving beetle is a very efficient predator. It has good eyesight and is a very fast swimmer; strong jaws and powerful front legs with gripping claws make it easy for this beetle to catch small fish and tadpoles. To add to its reputation as a predator, it can fly extremely well.

One of these beetles can seriously deplete the numbers of tadpoles or small fish in a garden pond, and it is not afraid of nipping a finger if it gets the chance. If the diving beetle is picked up it will make a frightening squeaking sound by squeezing air rapidly out of its body. When it has cleaned out one pond it will soon find its way to another.

The formidable-looking stag beetle has greatly enlarged mandibles which resemble the antlers of a deer. These are, however, only found in the males and they are used when sparring over a female or a particularly good rotting log. As the males grapple with each other, one will eventually be overcome and lose his position, leaving the other male triumphant. Fierce though they may appear, it is safe to handle this beetle as it is unable to nip fingers with its so-called antlers, which they display purely for show.

For these colourful, tropical longhorn beetles mating is a prolonged and cumbersome procedure. During this time the pair is vulnerable to attacks from predators.

With mandibles enlarged to resemble antlers, these male stag beetles are battling for the right to mate. The female is markedly smaller than the male and lacks his enlarged mouthparts.

This female praying mantis—the ultimate femme fatale—is eating her mate whilst still copulating. Although to our eyes this may seem offensive, the female gains a valuable meal vital to successful egg production.

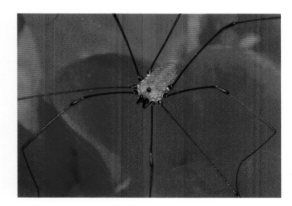

A harvestman is indeed a curious creature. Despite its appearance it is neither an insect nor a spider, although it is most closely related to the latter group; like arachnids, it has four pairs of legs.

The inflated throat sac of the male great frigate bird resembles a red balloon. The bird sits proudly on its chosen nesting bush waiting for a female to be enticed by his display.

Living up to their name, a pair of ambush bugs lie in wait on a flower head. This hapless fly has fallen into the trap and soon will be consumed by these deadly predators.

With slow but deliberate movements, this chameleon from Botswana walks gingerly across the hot sand. When it moves through the trees, its movements are almost imperceptible.

Some insects are capable of flying in tandem whilst paired and mating. The whole process of courtship and mating takes place on the wing for these syrphid flies from Brazil.

This bizarre collection of invertebrates, gathered together on a flower head, includes a mating pair of beetles and a crab spider with its prey. The red of the beetles indicates their unpalatable taste.

Jungle Oddities

South America provides zoologists with some very strange creatures for study. Many of the mammals are in classes unique to this continent and they are often found in remote and dangerous locations, making study very difficult.

Sloths are extraordinary mammals that live high in the tropical forests feeding on leaves. The sloth's stomach is divided into chambers, rather like those of ruminants, so that digestion of leaves can be done thoroughly. Much of the sloth's life is spent sleeping on a branch but when awake it hangs upside down, moving only very slowly from branch to branch. Its body temperature can drop as low as 24° Celsius (75° Fahrenheit), which few other mammals could cope with.

Once a week the sloth laboriously climbs down from a tree to the forest floor to deposit its droppings in a neat pile. Its tough, matted fur is greenish in appearance due to tiny algae growing on it; this colouring helps it to blend in with its treetop surroundings. On close examination, tiny larvae may sometimes be seen crawling through the fur. These are the caterpillars of the sloth moth, which eat algae. The skeleton of the sloth is unusual in its having one or two extra vertebrae, giving it greater flexibility when feeding whilst hanging upside down in trees.

The giant anteater, with its odd shape and disruptive camouflage, needs to eat around 30,000 insects a day in order to survive. To achieve this feat it has a long, flexible tongue covered with sticky projections. It can flick its tongue in and out of its mouth up to 150 times a minute, drawing ants and termites out of their nests in huge numbers. Strong front legs armed with sharp claws are used to tear into the ground or rotten tree stumps to expose the nests of its prey before the snout is pushed inside to get closer to its food.

Seen from the front the anteater seems to be a very slender animal, but from the side its flattened shape and thick bristly tail give it

The giant anteater is an extraordinary animal. Lacking teeth, it feeds on termites, gouging out termite mounds with its powerful claws and using its long snout and sticky tongue to extract them at the rate of thousands per minute.

an intimidating appearance. When confronted by a predator it does not face it head on but instead turns to the side to show the maximum extent of its body.

The nine-banded armadillo has a curiously armoured body. Ridges of bony plates cover the upper parts of the body, the limbs, and the tail. Only the underside is unprotected. Some species can roll into a tight ball when threatened, thus protecting its soft underside from attack. Powerful front legs, armed with strong claws, break up hard soil; the back legs kick the loose dirt out of the way. This allows the armadillo to locate invertebrate food and also to make a burrow to hide in.

Armadillos feed mainly on animals but will take plant food such as roots and bulbs as well, making them very successful creatures. Where their natural habitat has been cleared for agriculture, they have been able to adapt to feeding in arable land, inevitably making themselves unpopular with farmers due to the damage they do to crops.

Protected by a bony coat of mail, this nine-banded armadillo moves confidently over the forest floor. If a predator threatens, it simply rolls into a ball and remains so until the danger has passed.

With a name that conveys the impression of idleness, this three-toed sloth, an inhabitant of the tropical forests of South America, appears to live up to its name. Sloths move extremely slowly and have a correspondingly slow rate of metabolism.

Group Survival

Many mammals lead solitary lives but some have learnt to cooperate with one another so that all members of a community will benefit. Musk oxen, for example, will group together during winter storms to protect each other from driving snow and icy winds. Those in the centre of a group will be well protected from the weather by the large bodies of others but the animals on the outside will of course be exposed, on one side at least, to the worst of the weather. From time to time they shuffle around and change places so that all will get a chance of a little warmth.

Cooperating to protect the community from predators is also important. For instance, suricates, a type of rodent from southern Africa, are vulnerable to attack from eagles, jackals, small cats, and even baboons, so it is important that whilst some members of the group are feeding, tending young, or resting, others keep a sharp lookout for danger. Standing up on their hind legs gives them a good view all around; at the first sign of danger alarm calls can warn others in time for them all to make a quick escape.

In the field of animal behaviour we still have much to learn. The more we study the habits of the widely varied members of the animal kingdom the better our understanding is, naturally. However, there are still many areas which need more research. We know that the habits of animals are all important to their survival and that there is a sound reason for everything animals do; what eludes us at times are the reasons why certain animals behave in certain odd and curious ways.

The massed ranks of a musk ox herd present a formidable obstacle to would-be predators such as wolves. The musk oxen often form a defensive circle and will protect the young within it. They will also group together for protection from a winter storm.

"How diversified are the modes of life not only of incongruous but even of congenerous animals; and yet their specific distinctions are not more various than their propensities."
THE NATURAL HISTORY OF SELBORNE BY GILBERT WHITE, 1769

For up to a year after giving birth, a mother grey kangaroo will carry her youngster—known as a joey—around in her pouch. Marsupial young are born at a much earlier stage of development than placental mammals and hence they need prolonged care.

INDEX

*Page numbers in **bold-face** type indicate photo captions.*